at Play Sight *for piano*

The essential sight-reading course for elementary pianists

by Christine Brown

FABER **ff** MUSIC

Original edition © 1962/1987 EMI Music Publishing Ltd.
This edition © 2007 by EMI Music Publishing Ltd./Faber Music Ltd.
Music processed by Chris Hinkins
Text designed by Susan Clarke
Cover design by Sarah Theodosiou
Printed in England by Caligraving Ltd

ISBN10: 0-571-52506-7
EAN13: 978-0-571-52506-5

To buy Faber Music publications or to find out about the
full range of titles available please contact your local music retailer
or Faber Music sales enquiries:
Faber Music Ltd, Burnt Mill, Elizabeth Way, Harlow CM20 2HX
Tel: +44 (0) 1279 82 89 82 Fax: +44 (0) 1279 82 89 83
sales@fabermusic.com fabermusic.com

Contents

Introduction

The title *Play at Sight* is a positive one. It is essential that the playing of music at sight is presented in a positive way and not left to chance, as poor reading hampers musical development. The ability to play at sight is vitally important because it enables pupils to make better progress. They are able to practise more efficiently, learn new pieces more easily and explore music more widely. Sadly many of our pupils are poor readers. Often the reason is that they do very little reading, and as most people do not enjoy doing something they are not good at they do even less. So we have to break this vicious circle and provide them with a structured course which will allow them to make good progress in reading.

We have to face the fact that reading at sight a page of music, even at an elementary level, is a very complex process, much more complex than reading a page of words, and it has to be done in strict time! Nevertheless it is so important to develop this ability that we must try to unravel the complexities and help our pupils to become good readers.

What is involved in reading at sight? It demands a physical response to a visual symbol, so that the signs on the copy are translated into sounds. Some pupils are much quicker at making this response than others, but all can improve if the necessary skills are developed.

The first of these skills is the **knowledge of notation**. It is clear that we need a good knowledge of the signs if we are to translate them into sounds, so this is our starting point. It's often helpful to isolate pitch and rhythm at first although of course they have to be combined eventually. For instance in Part 1 of *Play at Sight* it is suggested that the pupil may clap the rhythm of a piece and then sing or say the names of the notes before he plays it on the piano. Knowledge of notation grows slowly, so in Part 1 the range of pitch is intentionally small until the pupil has gained some confidence. In Part 2 the range is gradually widened, but the pieces in Part 3 revert to a five-finger position when the pupil has to read both hands at once. Note values in Part 1 are limited to quavers, crotchets, minims, dotted minims and semibreves and the pupil is advised to clap the rhythm before attempting to play the piece. Dotted crotchets are introduced in Part 2 and semiquavers in Part 4, so there is plenty of variety in the rhythmic patterns even though the beat is always a crotchet.

The second essential skill is **knowledge of one's instrument**. A pupil may learn just one or two notes at first, so reading at sight is not usually a problem, but as the range of notes increases it is essential for him to be able to find the required notes without looking down at the keyboard or continuity will be lost when he plays. One way to develop this skill is to play exercises, scales, broken chords, arpeggios or even well-known pieces with eyes closed so the hands acquire knowledge of the geography of the keyboard and the player develops the confidence to keep to the Golden Rule 'Eyes on the music'. Another useful strategy is to prepare some 'Reading without looking down' exercises such as the following.

- Choose a key and place your right hand over the first five notes of the scale with your thumb on the key note. Then play without looking down at your fingers:

  1   3   2   4   5   3   1

- Choose a key and place your left hand over the first five notes of the scale, with your little finger on the key note. Then play without looking down at your fingers:

  5   3   2   4   1   3   5

If the pupil plays examples like these from different key notes he is in effect transposing as well as learning much about the geography of the keyboard.

The third essential skill for successful sight reading is **technique adequate to the task**. Pieces selected for reading must be well within a pupil's technical powers so that he can keep his eyes on the copy, keep in strict time and, above all, derive some pleasure from the activity. If the music is too difficult not only does the pupil fail to read it with ease but he may also develop bad habits. So the choice of material is crucial and for this reason all quaver movement in Parts 1 and 2 and all semiquaver movement in Part 4 is by step.

The **ability to grasp time patterns within a steady pulse** is the fourth skill necessary for good sight reading. Mathematical knowledge alone does not guarantee success as pupils who can tell you that there are four semiquavers in a crotchet cannot always clap accurately a crotchet followed by four semiquavers. There is no time to do sums while sight reading! Work is required to help the pupil to see time patterns as units, not as individual notes, just as in learning to read he comes to see words as a whole and not as individual letters. As soon as a pupil has learned two different note values, attempts to develop this skill can begin with simple clapping duets.

Rhythm work should continue on a regular basis with clapping duets in which the teacher keeps a steady pulse and with various games using flash cards of gradually increasing difficulty, each showing a bar of music.

The fifth essential skill for fluent sight reading is the **ability to memorise**. We tend to think that pupils are either good at reading or good at memorising, but in fact short-term memory is a necessary component for fluent reading too. The good reader is always memorising a bar or two ahead and although this short-term memory is limited it can be trained. One useful exercise is to place an envelope with a window over the first bar or two of the piece to be read, making sure the clefs, key and time signatures are visible, and then allow the pupil to look at it for as long as he wants before closing the book and asking him to play the bars from memory. Flash cards made from bars in *Play at Sight* are also useful and pupils can try to memorise these fragments more and more quickly. To encourage the pupil to look ahead as he reads try moving a postcard gradually from left to right to cover the bar he is about to play. This also prevents him from staring at the bar he has just played to discover what he did wrong or going back to correct a mistake, but watch his face – some pupils can feel distressed by this exercise.

There are no short cuts for making a pupil into a good reader but the acquisition of the five essential skills can be achieved through regular practice of the systematically graded material in *Play at Sight*. In addition those who work through this book will establish the habit of reading something new every day and will find pleasure in their increasing ability to read music at sight.

Christine Brown

Introducing three notes

First clap and count the rhythm, then place your fingers over the three notes and play the piece.

© 2007 by EMI Music Publishing Ltd./Faber Music Ltd.

Introducing more notes

Clap and count the rhythm first, then sing or say the names of the notes before you play.

Introducing ¾ time

First clap and count the rhythm, then place your fingers over the notes
required and play.

Some new starting notes

Clap and count the rhythm first, then sing or say the names of the notes
before you play.

Introducing crotchet rests

Clap each piece before you play, touching your lips and saying 'Sh' in the rests.

Introducing tied notes and $\frac{4}{4}$ time

First look for the tied notes, then clap and count before you play each piece.

part 1 The key of G

Place your fingers over all the notes required and stroke the F sharps
to help you to remember them.

The key of F

Place your fingers over all the notes required and stroke the B flats to help you to remember them.

The keys of G and F

Place your fingers over all the notes required, stroking the F sharps or
B flats before you play.

Crotchet and minim rests

Look for the rests, then clap each piece, saying 'Sh' in the crotchet rests
and 'Sh, sh' in the minim rests.

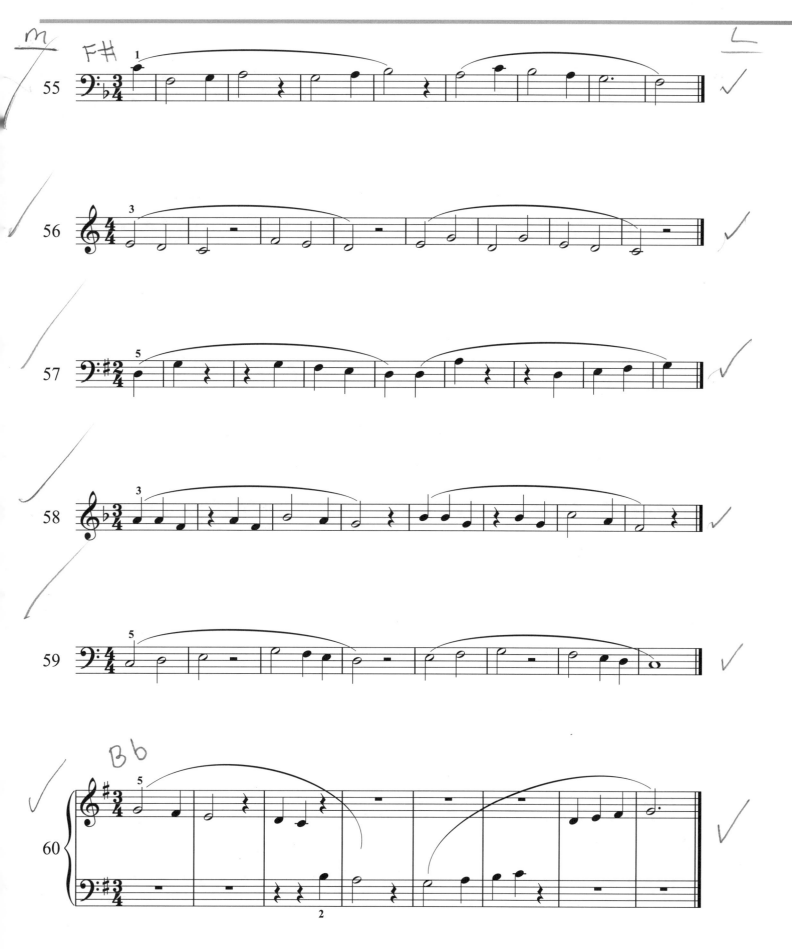

Introducing quavers

Set your metronome at ♩ = 60 and clap two bars of crotchets, followed by two bars of quavers. Then clap and count the rhythm of each piece before you play.

More quavers

First set your metronome at ♩ = 60 and clap the rhythm of each piece, keeping in
time with the metronome. Then place your fingers over the notes required and play.

Final reminders

1 Clap and count before you play.

2 Place your fingers over the notes required and stroke any F sharps or B flats.

Then play and enjoy the pieces.

Revision of keys C, G and F

Clap and count first. Then place your fingers over the notes required and sing or say the names of the notes in the correct rhythm.

1

2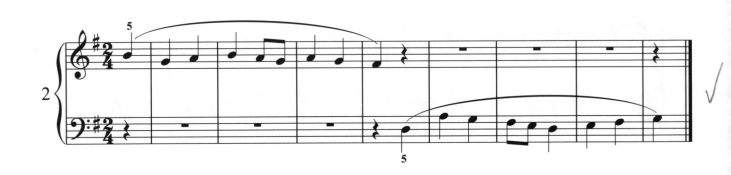

3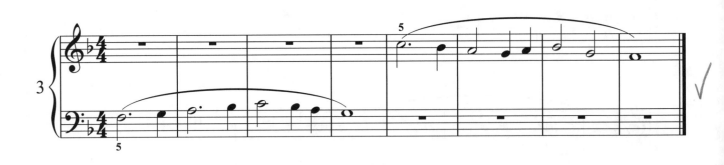

4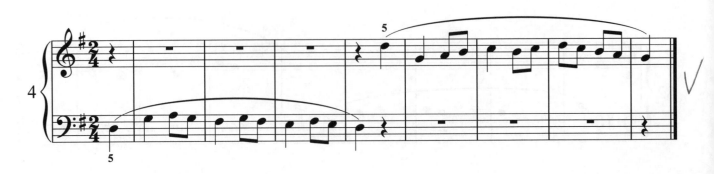

Look out for the tied notes!

First look for the tied notes, then clap and count before you play each piece.

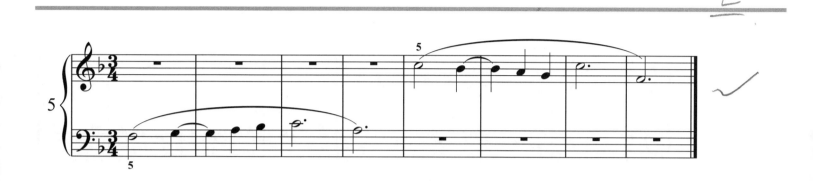

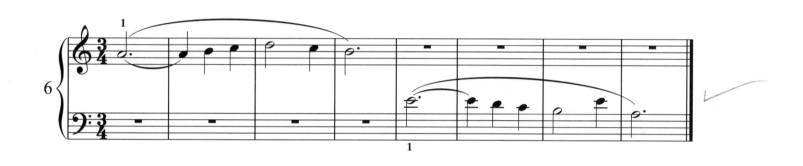

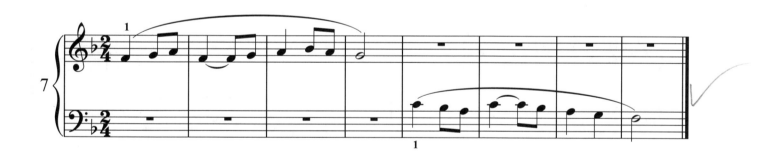

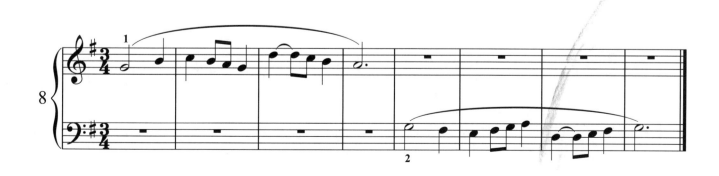

More crotchet and minim rests

Clap and count before you play. Make sure that you hear the silence in the rests.

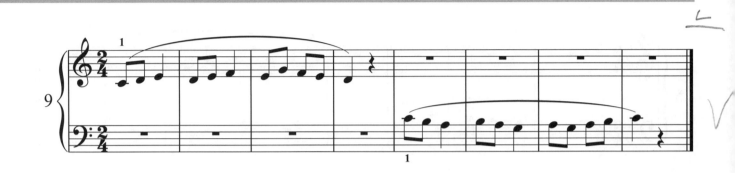

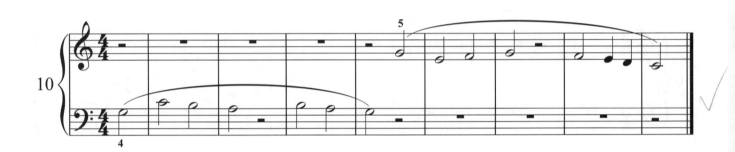

Introducing the dotted crotchet

Clap and count these duets with your teacher. Notice that in the top part, bars 3 and 4 look different but sound alike.

part
2

More dotted crotchets

Clap and count first. Then sing or say the names of the notes
in the correct rhythm.

Even more dotted crotchets

Clap and count before you play and make sure that you hear the silence in the rests.

Extensions beyond five notes

Clap and count first. Then place your fingers over the opening notes
of each phrase and look ahead to see where the extension comes.

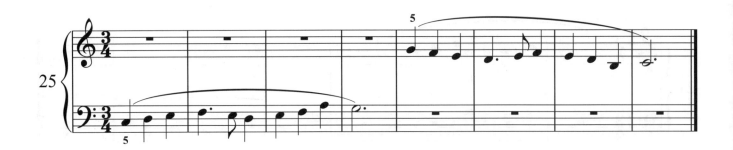

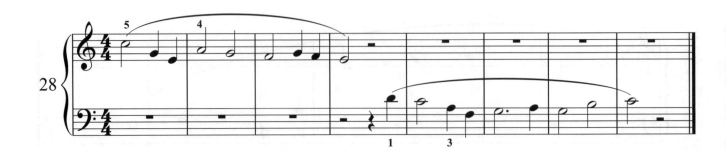

More extensions

Clap and count first. Then look for the extensions and practise moving
your fingers the correct distance without looking down at your hands.

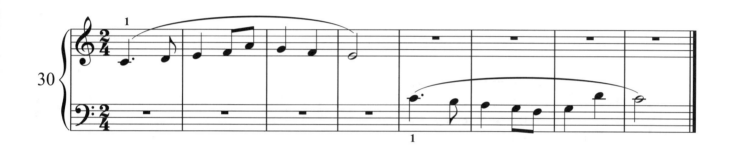

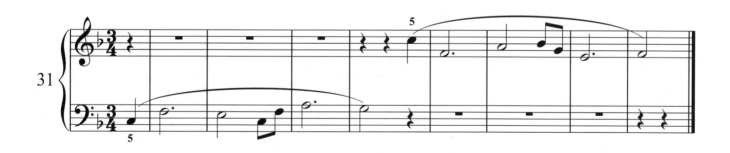

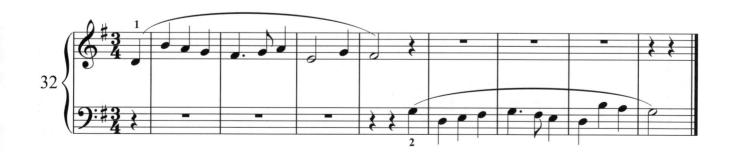

Introducing a new time pattern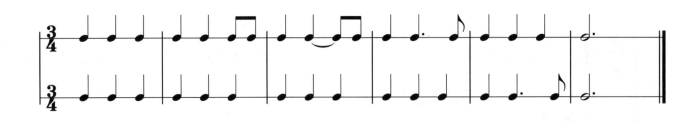

Clap and count this duet with your teacher. Which two bars sound alike?
Now clap and count each piece before you play.

33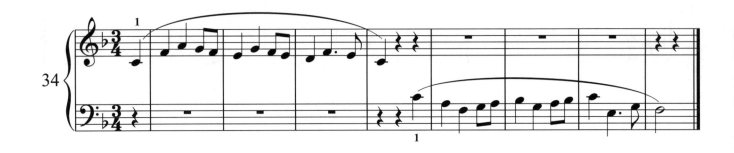

34

35

36

Some wider extensions

Clap and count first, then place your fingers over the opening notes of each
phrase and silently rehearse the extensions without looking down at your hands.

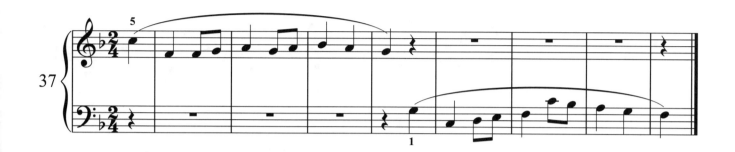

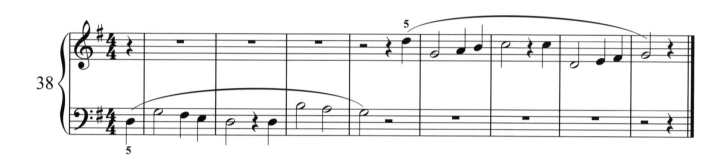

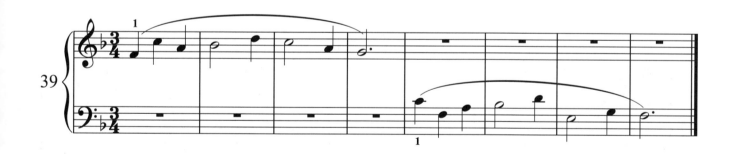

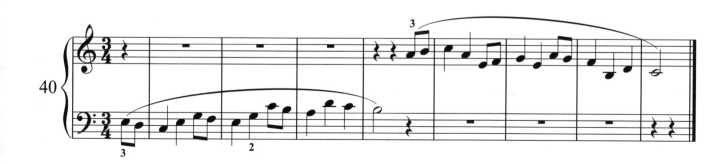

Introducing octave leaps

Play the following exercises to help yourself to play an octave leap without looking down at your hands. If you look down you may lose your place!

30

Final reminders

1 Clap and count before you play.
2 Make sure that you hear the silence in the rests.
3 Place your fingers over the opening notes of each phrase and stroke any F sharps
  or B flats needed.
4 Prepare for any extensions so that you do not have to look down at your hands.

Now enjoy playing these pieces.

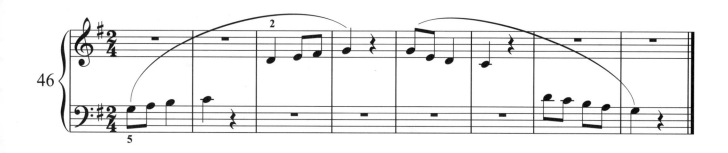

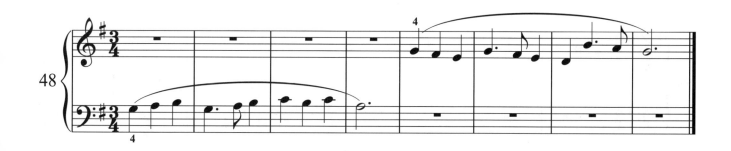

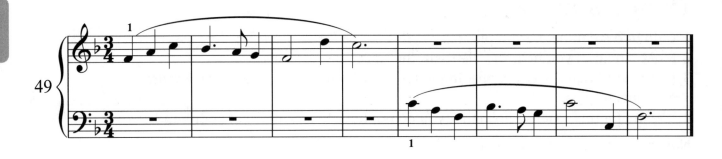

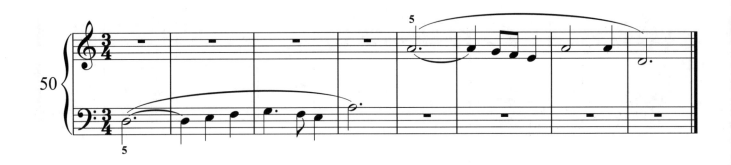

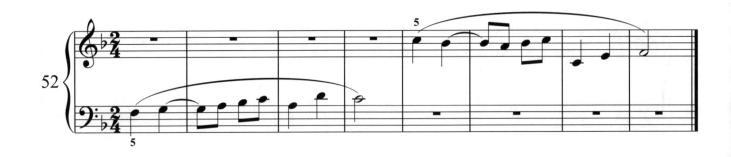

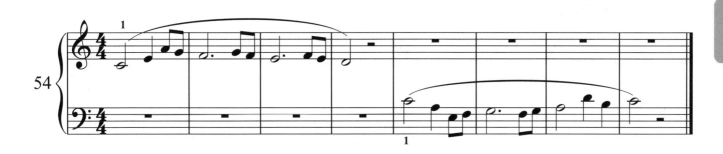

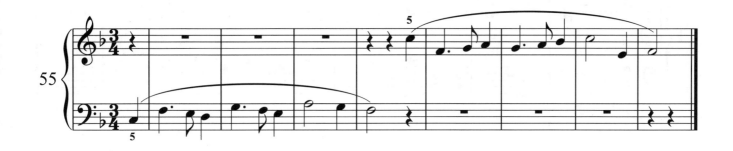

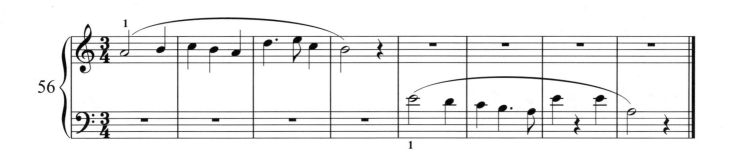

The key of C

Count aloud and tap out the rhythm of each piece using both hands, right hand on right knee and left hand on left knee. Then place your fingers over the notes required and play without looking down at your hands.

The key of G

Count aloud and tap out the rhythm of each piece using both hands.
Then place your fingers over the notes required, remembering to
stroke any F sharps, and play without looking down at your hands.

29/1 ✓ 9

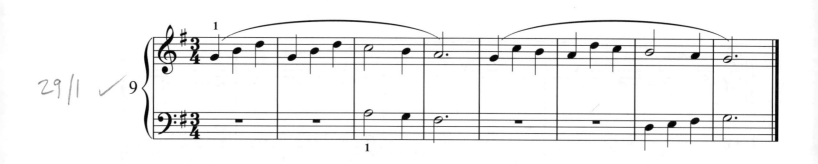

10

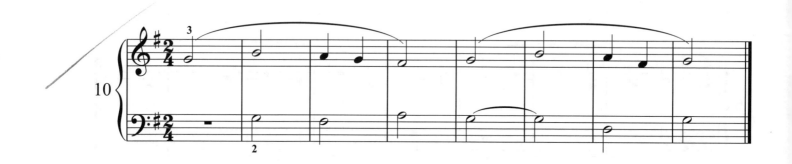

11

12

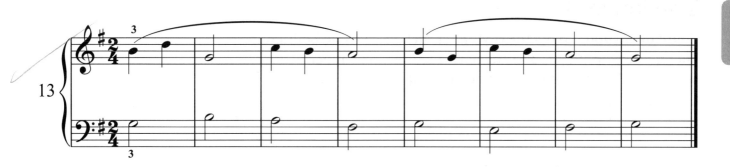

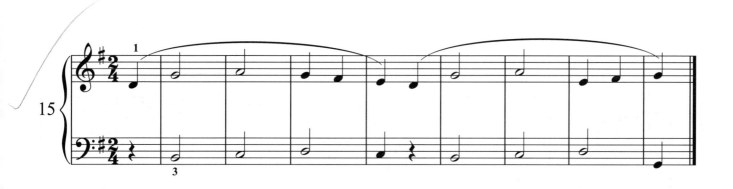

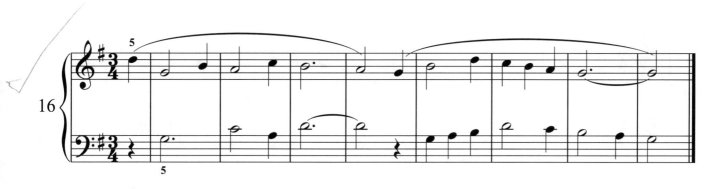

The key of F

Count aloud and tap out the rhythm of each piece using both hands.
Then place your fingers over the notes required, remembering to
stroke any B flats, and play without looking down at your hands.

12/2 ✓

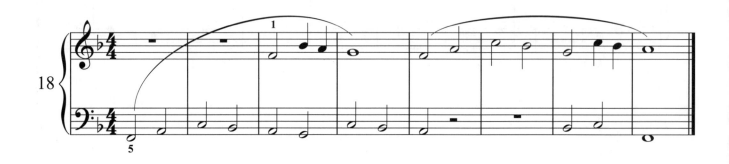

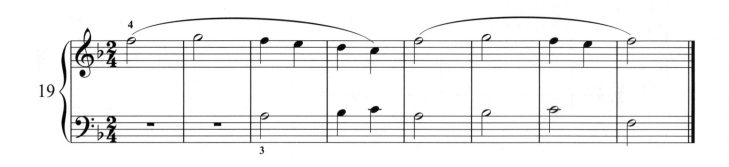

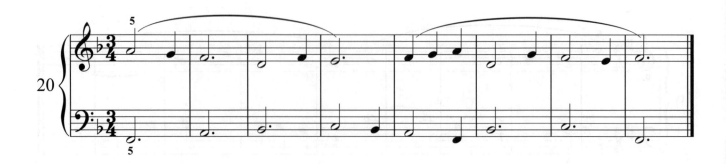

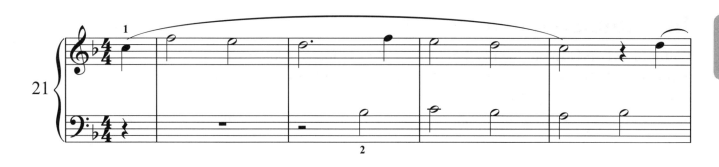

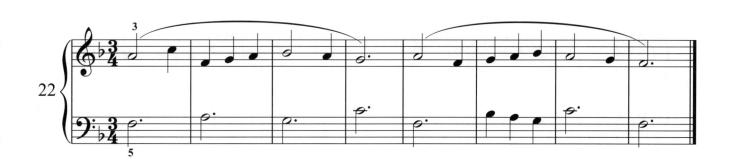

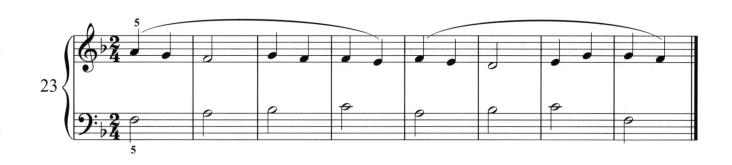

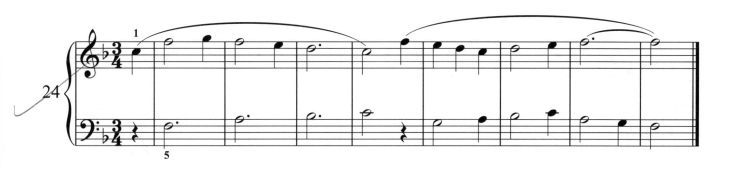

Introducing quavers

Count aloud and tap out the rhythm of each piece before you play.
Remember to stroke any F sharps or B flats needed before you start
and keep your eyes on the music.

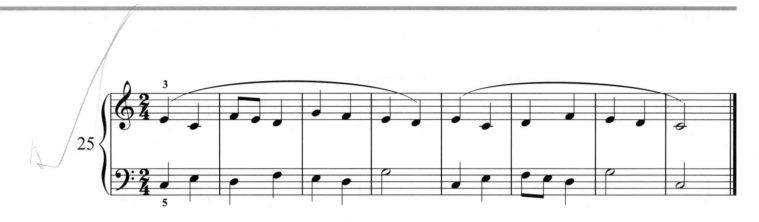

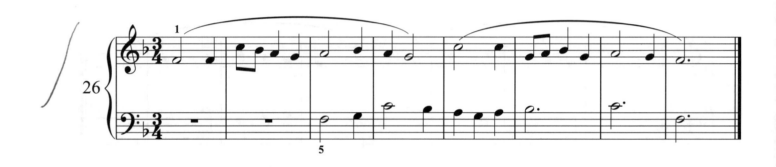

29
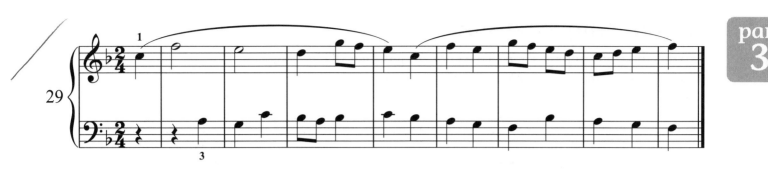

30

31

32

Introducing extensions

part 3

Tap out the rhythm first. Then place your fingers over the opening
notes of each phrase and look ahead to see where the extensions come.

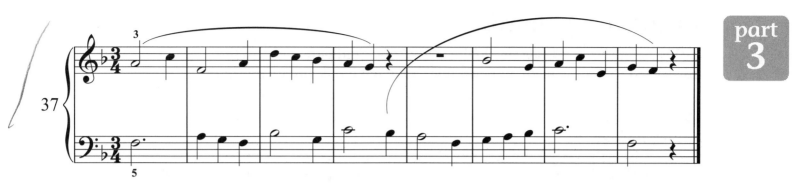

37

38

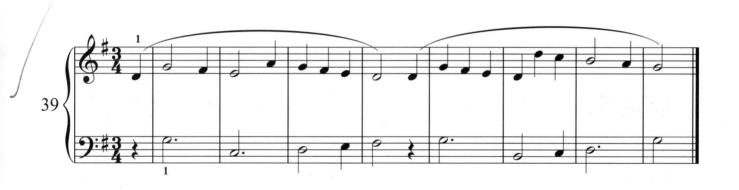

39

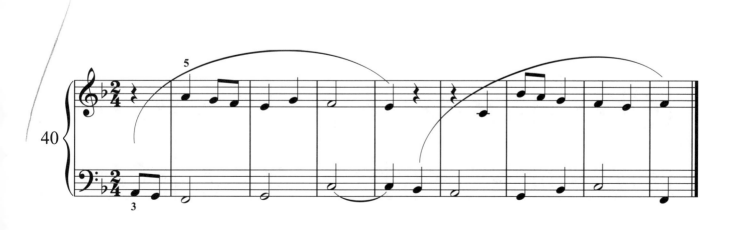

40

Introducing chords

First look for the chords and using the correct fingering play them 'in the air'. Then tap out the piece and play it without looking down at your hands.

41

42

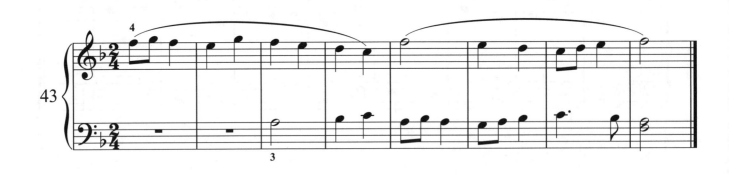

43

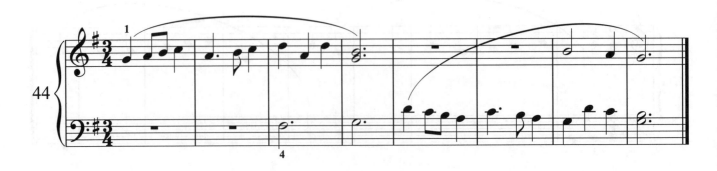

44

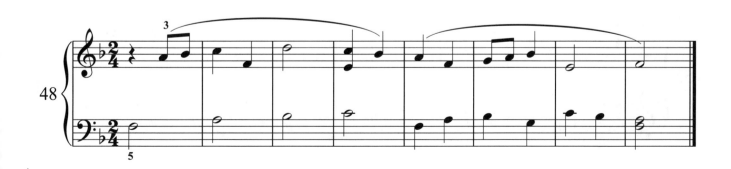

Introducing changing clefs

Tap out the rhythm first. Then check the clefs and place your fingers over the notes required, noticing any extensions so that you can play without looking down at your hands.

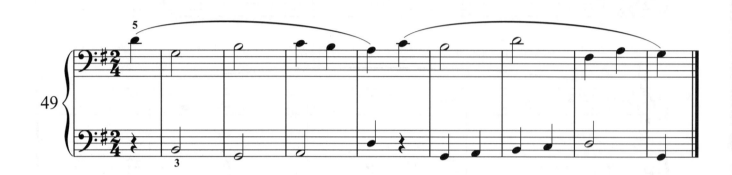

49

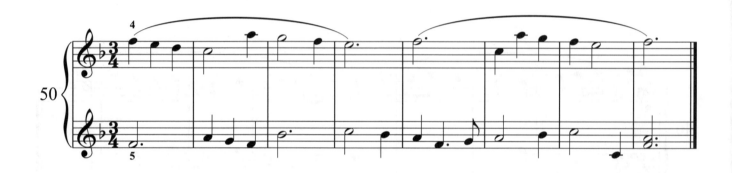

50

51

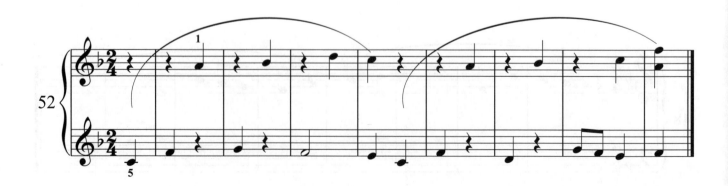

52

Final reminders

1 Tap out the rhythm of each piece on your knees before you play.
2 Make sure that you hear the silence in the rests.
3 Check the clefs.
4 Play any chords 'in the air', with the correct fingering.
5 Place your fingers over the opening notes and stroke any F sharps or B flats required.
6 Prepare for any extensions so that you do not have to look down at your hands.

Now you can enjoy playing the pieces!

The key of C major

Every major key has a relative minor which shares its key signature.
So every key signature can stand for two keys, one major and one minor.
There are no sharps or flats in the key signature of C major. Tap out each
piece on your knees then play without looking down at your hands.

The key of A minor

There are no sharps or flats in the key signature of A minor, but there
may be F sharps and G sharps in the piece. Tap out each piece first,
then place your fingers over the notes required, stroking any sharps so
that you remember them.

The key of G major

The key signature of G major is F sharp. Tap out each piece first, then place your fingers over the notes required, stroking the F sharps and noticing any extensions.

The key of E minor

The key signature of E minor is F sharp, the same as that of G major, but there may be C sharps and D sharps in the piece as well. Tap out each piece first, then place your fingers over the notes required, stroking any sharps so that you remember them.

The key of F major

The key signature of F major is B flat. Tap out each piece first, then place your fingers over the notes required, stroking the B flats and noticing any extensions.

The key of D minor

The key signature of D minor is B flat, the same as that of F major, but there may be C sharps in the piece as well. Tap out each piece first, then place your fingers over the notes required, stroking any B flats and C sharps so that you remember them.

Changes of position in the right hand

First tap out the rhythm and decide on the key of the piece. Then place your left hand in position over the required notes. Next place your right hand in position for the first phrase and then move it to the position for the second phrase. Now that you have rehearsed the move you will not need to look down at your hands when you play.

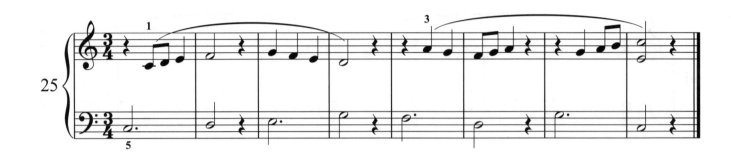

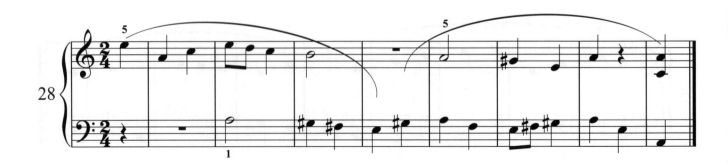

Changes of position in the left hand

First tap out the rhythm and decide on the key of the piece. Then place your right hand in position over the required notes. Next place your left hand in position for the first phrase and then move it to the position for the second phrase. Now that you have rehearsed the move you will not need to look down at your hands when you play.

Changes of position in both hands

First tap out the rhythm and decide on the key of the piece. Then silently rehearse the changes of position with both hands before you play.

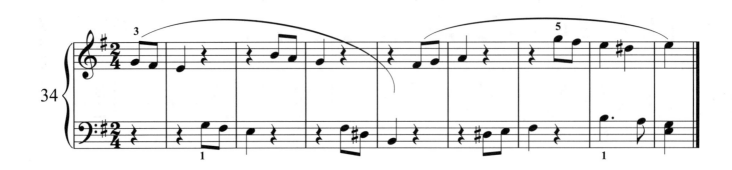

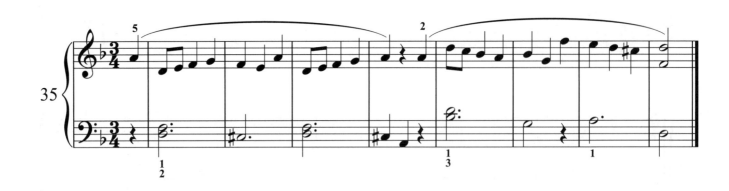

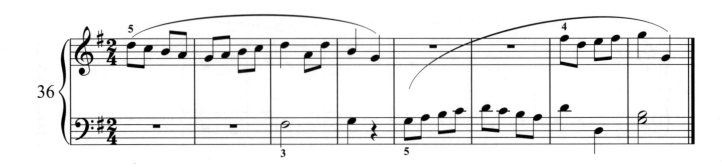

Introducing slurs and staccato

First tap out the rhythm on your knees, observing the slurs and staccato notes. Then decide on the key and silently rehearse the changes of position before you play.

Introducing semiquavers

First set your metronome at ♩ = 60 and clap two bars of crotchets, two of quavers and two of semiquavers. Then tap out on your knees the rhythm of each piece before you play it.

Introducing expression marks

First tap out the rhythm on your knees, following the expression marks in your tapping. Then rehearse any changes of position before you play.

Final reminders

1 Tap out the rhythm on your knees observing slurs, staccato and expression marks.
2 Make sure that you hear the silence in the rests.
3 Decide on the key.
4 Check the clefs.
5 Play any chords 'in the air' using the correct fingering.
6 Place your fingers over the opening notes and stroke any black notes required.
7 Notice any extensions and silently rehearse any changes of position so that you
   do not have to look down at your hands.

Now you can enjoy playing the pieces!

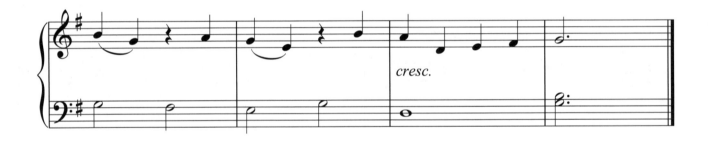